THE LIFE CYCLE OF A

LADYBUG

By L. L. Owens

The Child's World

Published by The Child's World®
1980 Lookout Drive
Mankato, MN 56003-1705
800-599-READ
www.childsworld.com

The Child's World®: Mary Berendes, Publishing Director
The Design Lab: Kathleen Petelinsek, design
Red Line Editorial: Editorial direction

Photographs ©: iStockphoto, cover (top right, bottom left, bottom right), 1 (top right, bottom left, bottom right), 3; Robert Grubba/iStockphoto, cover (top left), 1 (top left); Henrik Larsson/Shutterstock Images, 5, 31 (top); Shutterstock Images, 6, 10, 22; Andrea Gingerich/iStockphoto, 9; Photolibrary, 13; James Benet/iStockphoto, 14, 30 (bottom); D. Kucharski & K. Kucharska/Shutterstock Images, 17; 123RF, 18, 31 (bottom); Christine vanReeuwyk/Shutterstock Images, 21; Steve Shoup/Shutterstock Images, 25; Hans Pfletschinger/Photolibrary, 26, 30 (top); Sebastian Knight/Shutterstock Images, 29

ISBN: 978-1-60973-189-2
LCCN: 2011927739

Printed in the United States of America
Mankato, MN
July 2011
PA02089

LIFE CYCLES

Every living thing has a life cycle. A life cycle is the steps a living thing goes through as it grows and changes. Humans have a life cycle. Animals have a life cycle. Plants have a life cycle, too.

A cycle is something that happens over and over again. A life cycle begins with the start of a new life. It continues as a plant or creature grows. And it keeps going as one living thing creates another, or **reproduces**— and the cycle starts over again.

A ladybug's life cycle has four main steps: egg, **larva**, **pupa**, and adult ladybug.

Adult ladybugs crawl and fly all around as they look for food and mates.

Ladybugs come in many colors, including yellow and pink.

LADYBUGS

Ladybugs are flying insects. An insect is a six-legged animal without a backbone. Instead, a hard covering protects its soft body. Ladybugs are a type of beetle. These insects usually have four wings.

About 5,000 types of ladybugs live around the world. They mostly live in warm places. Different kinds of ladybugs come in many colors and patterns. You have probably seen one of the most common types—it is red with seven black spots. This kind is called the seven-spotted lady beetle.

A LADYBUG'S BODY

Like other insects, ladybugs have three main body parts: head, **thorax**, and **abdomen**. Males and females look alike, but females are usually bigger.

On its tiny head are two eyes, a pair of strong jaws, and two **antennae**. The antennae are feelers. They help the ladybug sense its surroundings through smell, taste, and touch.

Their eyes sense light and dark, but ladybugs cannot see very well.

To fly, a ladybug raises its outer wings. Underneath are thin flight wings, which lift the bug into the air.

A ladybug's six legs and four wings are part of the thorax. The outer pair of wings— the ones with the spots—act as a protective shell. The inner pair, the flight wings, stay covered until needed. In flight, a ladybug's wings beat 85 times per second.

The abdomen is the rear part of an insect's body. This is where food is digested. You can catch a glimpse of the abdomen when a ladybug spreads its wings.

HATCHING

In their life cycle, ladybugs go through a process of change called **metamorphosis**. The cycle begins inside an egg. In the spring, a female deposits a few clusters of 15 or more tiny eggs on the underside of several plant leaves. The yellow, oval-shaped eggs stick to the leaf, standing on one end.

Inside an egg grows a tiny **embryo**, or baby ladybug. There is also a yolk inside the egg. The embryo gets the nutrients it needs from the yolk. The egg turns white or gray three to five days before **hatching** occurs.

Ladybugs will lay egg clusters on leaves, tree bark, or plant stems.

A larva changes from white to black.

NEW LADYBUG

After hatching, a baby ladybug is called a larva. A single larva is about the size of a pinhead.

Male and female larvae look alike. They have six legs and two antennae, but they do not look like adult ladybugs. The larvae look a little like young alligators. Newly hatched larvae are hungry!

Female ladybugs do not stay with their eggs, so the larvae must find their own food. Larvae can't yet fly. But these hungry insects can crawl. They cling to plants as they hunt for food.

Ladybugs at any age will eat mites. But they eat a lot of aphids, too. Aphids are tiny bugs that feed on juices from plants.

Hungry larvae eat aphids.

A pupa can be light orange, black, gray, brown, or white.

A ladybug larva grows quickly. But its skin does not grow with it. A larva must shed its skin, or **molt**, to get bigger. It breaks out of its old skin. Underneath is new skin that hardens into a new protective casing.

Within two to four weeks, the ladybug larva has shed its skin about three or four times. It has grown enough to change again. It attaches itself to a plant leaf or stem. It sheds its skin one last time. It is now a pupa. A protective casing forms around the pupa.

AN ADULT EMERGES

The pupa does not move or eat. It uses stored energy from all the food it ate as a larva. During this time, its body is changing. Inside the pupa's protective casing, wings and other adult body parts are forming. After about a week, the casing splits open and an adult ladybug emerges. It comes out looking very pale. Its wings are soft and wet.

The ladybug's spots begin to appear over the next few hours. Soon the wings dry and darken. Less than a day later, the new ladybug looks like an adult ladybug. Metamorphosis is complete!

A new adult ladybug is soft and pale before its body hardens and its colors become darker.

A ladybug's bright colors show **predators** that it might taste bad.

An adult ladybug's instincts help it find food and shelter. It must keep itself safe from predators. A ladybug's bright colors help. Its colors warn predators that the ladybug does not taste good. But if a crow or a dragonfly is near, a ladybug might protect itself by playing dead. Or it might release a smell the predator does not like.

A ladybug can live for a year or two. To make it through a winter, a group of ladybugs might gather in a log, beneath a pile of leaves, or inside a wall. They go into a deep sleep called **hibernation**, waking up in spring.

Ladybugs often mate in the spring. A female ladybug releases a scent that attracts a male. Some female ladybugs mate with many males. After mating, the male and the female separate.

A group of ladybugs finds a sheltered place to hibernate during the winter.

When the eggs hatch, the larvae will begin to eat aphids.

LAYING EGGS

A female ladybug lays her egg clusters in
several safe spots. A good place is under
the leaves of plants that aphids like to eat. A
ladybug's role as parent ends here. She does
not stay with her eggs. She will lay more eggs,
though—up to 1,000 during her lifetime.

If the eggs stay safe, they will hatch about
one week later. Hungry larvae crawl out.
They eat aphids and other bugs. And the life
cycle of the ladybug continues.

Many farmers like ladybugs. Ladybugs eat bugs that destroy crops.

LIFE CYCLE DIAGRAM

Egg

Larva

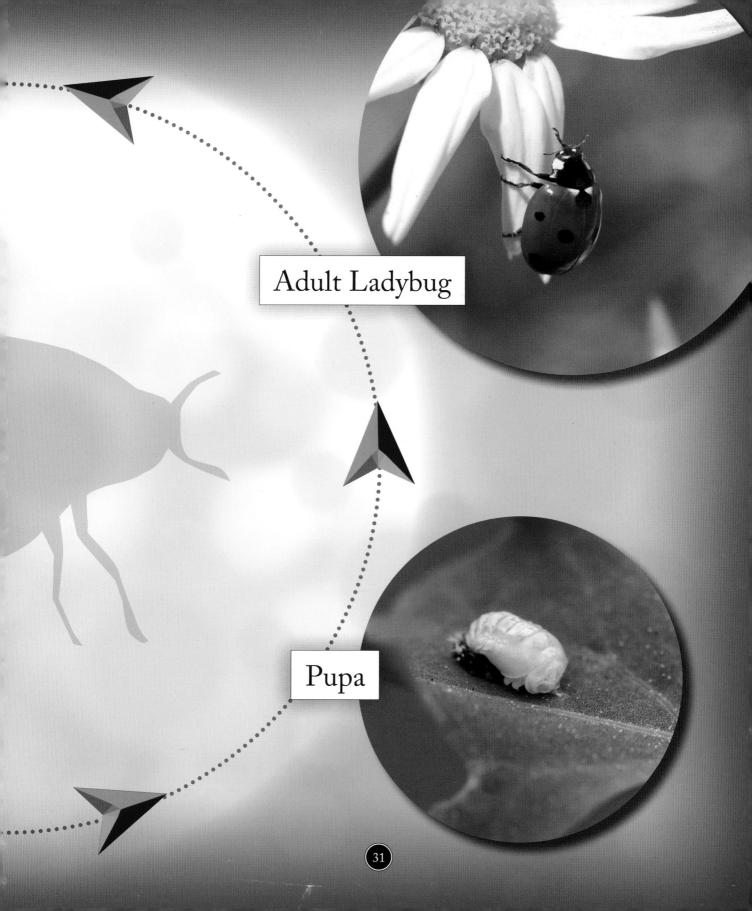

Adult Ladybug

Pupa

Web Sites

Visit our Web site for links about the life cycle of a ladybug: **childsworld.com/links**

Note to Parents, Teachers, and Librarians: We routinely verify our Web links to make sure they are safe and active sites. So encourage your readers to check them out!

Books

Kalman, Bobbie. *Animal Life Cycles: Growing and Changing.* New York: Crabtree Publishing Company, 2006.

Ross, Michael Elsohn. *Life Cycles.* Brookfield, CT: Millbrook Press, 2001.

Slade, Suzanne. *Ladybugs.* New York: PowerKids Press, 2008.

Glossary

abdomen (AB-duh-muhn): The abdomen is the rear section of an insect's body. A ladybug's food is digested in the abdomen.

antennae (an-TEN-ee): Antennae are thin feelers on an insect's head. A ladybug uses its antennae to smell, taste, and touch.

embryo (EM-bree-oh): An embryo is an organism in the early stages of growth. Inside a ladybug egg is a tiny embryo.

hatching (HACH-ing): Hatching is when something breaks out of its egg. Ladybug eggs turn white or gray just before hatching.

hibernation (hye-bur-NAY-shun): Hibernation is a state of very deep sleep, with slowed breathing and heartbeat. During the winter, a ladybug goes into hibernation.

larva (LAR-vuh): A larva is an animal soon after hatching that looks very different from its parents. A ladybug larva is very hungry and eats many aphids.

metamorphosis (met-uh-MOR-fuh-siss): Metamorphosis is the series of changes some animals go through between hatching and adulthood. Ladybugs look very different at each stage of metamorphosis.

molt (molt): To molt is to shed old skin and grow new skin. A ladybug larva will molt as it grows.

predators (PRED-uh-turs): Predators are animals that hunt and eat other animals. Ladybugs might play dead to stay safe from predators.

pupa (PYOO-puh): A pupa is an insect in the life cycle stage between larva and adult. A ladybug pupa often attaches to a leaf or a stem.

reproduces (re-pruh-DOOS-ez): If an animal or plant reproduces, it produces offspring. A ladybug pair reproduces and creates new ladybugs.

thorax (THOR-aks): A thorax is the middle section of an insect's body. A ladybug's legs and wings grow from the thorax.